THE BOOK OF ANSWERS
CAROL BOLT

BANTAM BOOKS

LONDON · NEW YORK · TORONTO · SYDNEY · AUCKLAND

THE BOOK OF ANSWERS
A BANTAM BOOK: ISBN 9780553813548

First publication in Great Britain

PRINTING HISTORY
Bantam Books edition published 2000

19 20

Set in Trajan by Falcon Oast Graphic Art.

Bantam Books are published by Transworld Publishers,
61–63 Uxbridge Road, London W5 5SA,
a division of The Random House Group Ltd

Addresses for Random House Group Ltd companies outside the UK
can be found at: www.randomhouse.co.uk
The Random House Group Ltd Reg. No. 954009

The Random House Group Limited makes every effort to ensure that the papers
used in its books are made from trees that have been legally sourced from well-managed
and credibly certified forests. Our paper procurement policy can be found at:
www.randomhouse.co.uk/paper.htm

Reproduced, printed and bound in Great Britain
by Mackays of Chatham, Chatham, Kent.

THE BOOK OF ANSWERS

1. Hold the closed book in your hand, on your lap or on a table.

2. Take ten or fifteen seconds to concentrate on your question. Questions should be phrased in the following style: 'Is the job I'm applying for the right one?' or, 'Should I travel this weekend?'

3. While visualizing or speaking your question (one question at a time), place one hand palm down on the book's front cover and stroke the edge of the pages, back to front.

4. When you sense the time is right, simply open the book and there will be your answer.

5. Repeat the process for as many questions as you have.

INTRIGUING AND INSPIRING,
THE BOOK OF ANSWERS HAS THE SOLUTION TO
YOUR EVERY QUESTION!

Carol Bolt is a professional artist living in Seattle.
This is her first book.

YOUR ACTIONS WILL
IMPROVE THINGS

DON'T BET ON IT

ADOPT AN
ADVENTUROUS ATTITUDE

FOLLOW THE ADVICE
OF THE EXPERTS

YOU COULD FIND YOURSELF
UNABLE TO COMPROMISE

FOCUS ON YOUR HOME LIFE

INVESTIGATE AND THEN ENJOY IT

DEFINITELY

IT WILL REMAIN UNPREDICTABLE

ABSOLUTELY NOT

EXPLORE IT
WITH PLAYFUL CURIOSITY

BE DELIGHTFULLY SURE OF IT

BETTER TO WAIT

IT SEEMS ASSURED

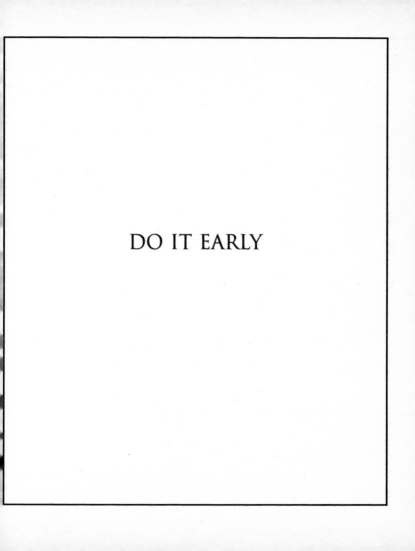

DO IT EARLY

KEEP IT TO YOURSELF

STARTLING EVENTS
MAY OCCUR AS A RESULT

THE ANSWER MAY COME TO YOU
IN ANOTHER LANGUAGE

YOU WILL NEED
TO ACCOMMODATE

DOUBT IT

IT WILL BRING GOOD LUCK

BE PATIENT

YOU WILL FIND OUT EVERYTHING
YOU'LL NEED TO KNOW

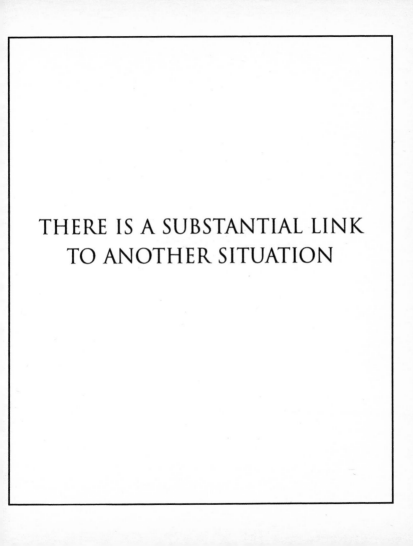

THERE IS A SUBSTANTIAL LINK
TO ANOTHER SITUATION

WATCH AND SEE WHAT HAPPENS

IT WILL AFFECT
HOW OTHERS SEE YOU

YOU'LL BE HAPPY YOU DID

GET IT IN WRITING

UNFAVOURABLE AT THIS TIME

UPGRADE ANY WAY YOU CAN

IF YOU DO AS YOU'RE TOLD

IF IT'S DONE WELL;
IF NOT, DON'T DO IT AT ALL

DON'T ASK FOR ANY MORE
AT THIS TIME

AVOID THE FIRST SOLUTION

YOU'LL GET THE FINAL WORD

PROCEED AT A MORE
RELAXED PACE

THE BEST SOLUTION
MAY NOT BE THE OBVIOUS ONE

REMAIN FLEXIBLE

THAT'S OUT OF YOUR CONTROL

PROVIDED YOU SAY
'THANK YOU'

ENJOY THE EXPERIENCE

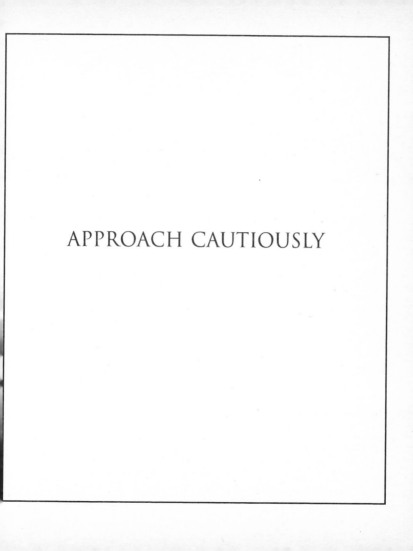

APPROACH CAUTIOUSLY

PAY ATTENTION TO THE DETAILS

WATCH YOUR STEP AS YOU GO

SPEAK UP ABOUT IT

DON'T HESITATE

THIS IS A GOOD TIME TO
MAKE A NEW PLAN

MOVE ON

THERE IS NO GUARANTEE

THE CIRCUMSTANCES
WILL CHANGE VERY QUICKLY

DON'T GET CAUGHT UP
IN YOUR EMOTIONS

SHIFT YOUR FOCUS

IT IS SIGNIFICANT

REPRIORITIZE
WHAT IS IMPORTANT

MAKE A LIST OF WHY NOT

DON'T WAIT

IT IS SOMETHING
YOU WON'T FORGET

EXPECT TO SETTLE

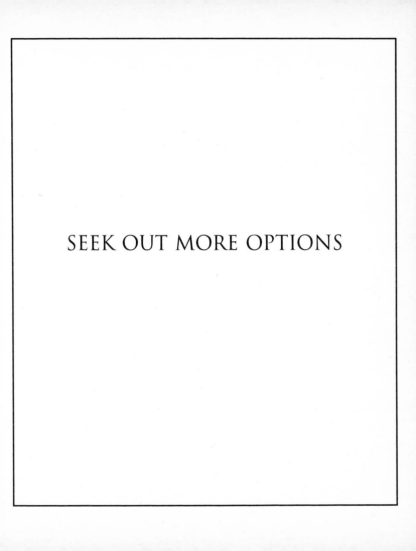

SEEK OUT MORE OPTIONS

FOLLOW THROUGH
ON YOUR OBLIGATIONS

DEAL WITH IT LATER

FOLLOW SOMEONE ELSE'S LEAD

MAKE A LIST OF WHY

TAKE A CHANCE

ACCEPT A CHANGE
TO YOUR ROUTINE

YOU'LL NEED TO TAKE
THE INITIATIVE

YOU'LL HAVE TO COMPROMISE

YOU'LL NEED
MORE INFORMATION

TRUST YOUR
ORIGINAL THOUGHT

IT WILL CREATE A STIR

REMOVE YOUR OWN OBSTACLES

IT WOULD BE BETTER
TO FOCUS ON YOUR WORK

IT WILL BE A PLEASURE

BE MORE GENEROUS

BET ON IT

FINISH SOMETHING ELSE FIRST

YOU MAY HAVE OPPOSITION

YOU ARE TOO CLOSE TO SEE

THE SITUATION IS UNCLEAR

A SUBSTANTIAL EFFORT
WILL BE REQUIRED

ALLOW YOURSELF TO REST FIRST

THE CHANCE WILL NOT
COME AGAIN SOON

RECONSIDER YOUR APPROACH

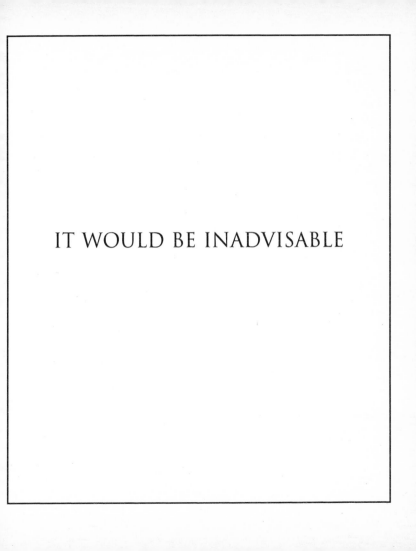

IT WOULD BE INADVISABLE

WAIT FOR A BETTER OFFER

SETTLE IT SOON

YES,
BUT DON'T FORCE IT

GET A CLEARER VIEW

TAKE A CHANCE

NOW YOU CAN

DON'T OVERDO IT

IT WILL SUSTAIN YOU

IT'LL COST YOU

IT IS SURE TO MAKE THINGS
INTERESTING

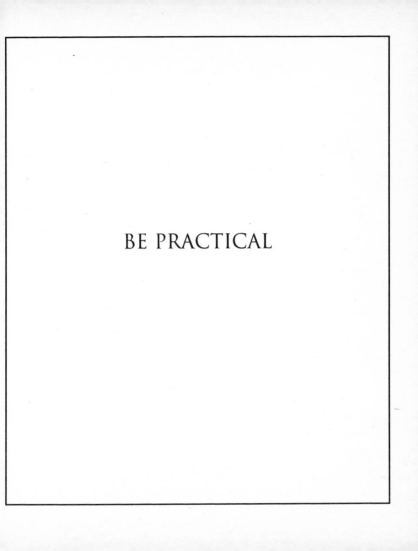

BE PRACTICAL

SAVE YOUR ENERGY

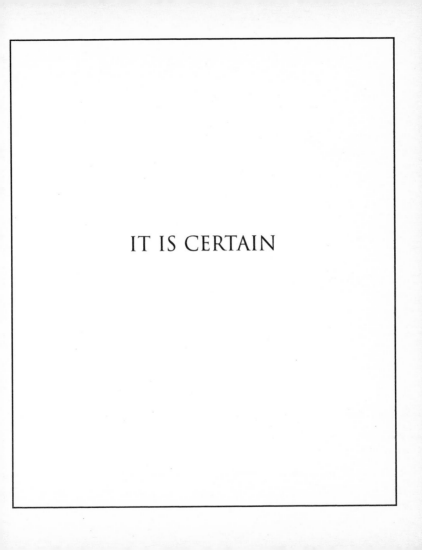

IT IS CERTAIN

IT IS UNCERTAIN

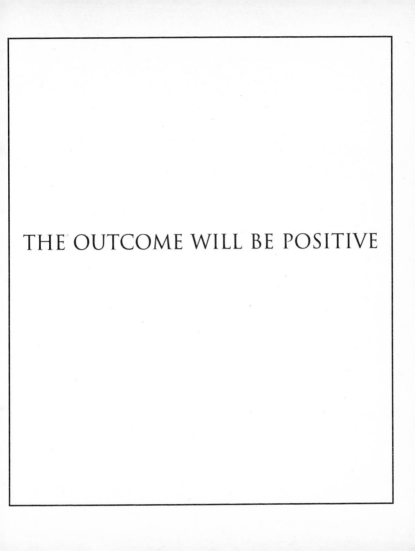

THE OUTCOME WILL BE POSITIVE

NO MATTER WHAT

YOU MAY HAVE TO DROP
OTHER THINGS

DON'T BE CONCERNED

PREPARE FOR THE UNEXPECTED

IT IS NOT SIGNIFICANT

TELL SOMEONE
WHAT IT MEANS TO YOU

WHATEVER YOU DO
THE RESULTS WILL BE LASTING

KEEP AN OPEN MIND

IT'S A GOOD TIME
TO MAKE PLANS

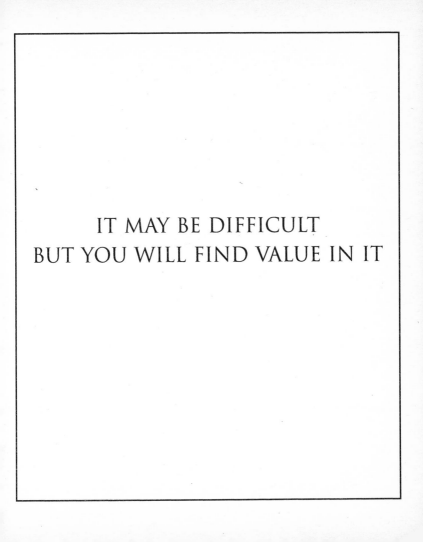

IT MAY BE DIFFICULT
BUT YOU WILL FIND VALUE IN IT

IT IS WORTH THE TROUBLE

THERE WILL BE OBSTACLES
TO OVERCOME

RELATED ISSUES MAY SURFACE

YOU ARE SURE TO HAVE SUPPORT

ASSISTANCE WOULD MAKE
YOUR PROGRESS
A SUCCESS

COLLABORATION
WILL BE THE KEY

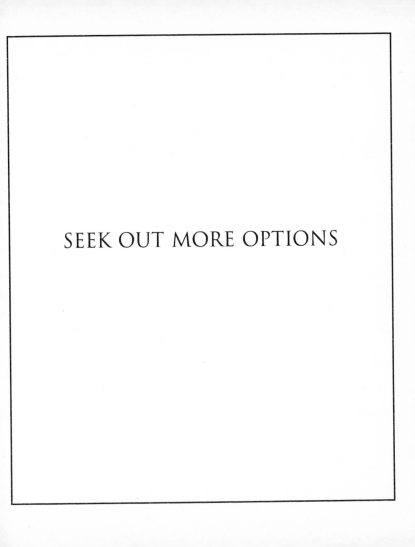

SEEK OUT MORE OPTIONS

TAKE CHARGE

IT CANNOT FAIL

YOU MUST ACT NOW

RESPECT THE RULES

GENTLE PERSISTENCE
WILL PAY OFF

YOU WILL NOT BE DISAPPOINTED

IT MAY ALREADY BE
A DONE DEAL

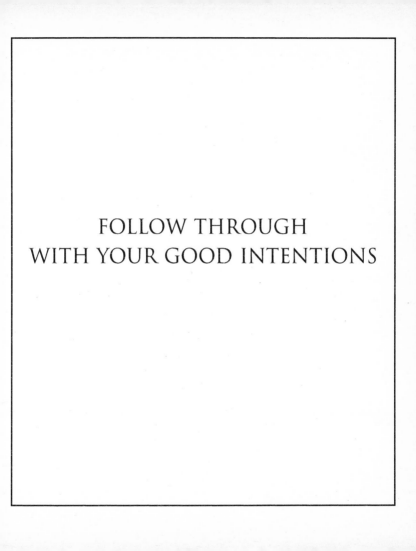

FOLLOW THROUGH
WITH YOUR GOOD INTENTIONS

TAKE MORE TIME TO DECIDE

DON'T BE PRESSURED
INTO ACTING TOO QUICKLY

DON'T IGNORE THE OBVIOUS

IF YOU DON'T RESIST

IT'S NOT WORTH A STRUGGLE

DON'T FORGET TO HAVE FUN

DON'T DOUBT IT

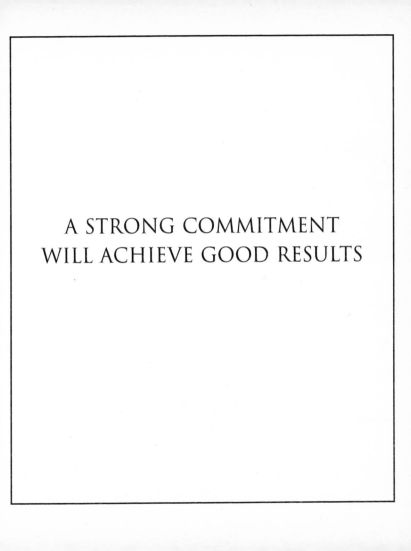

A STRONG COMMITMENT
WILL ACHIEVE GOOD RESULTS

TRY A MORE UNLIKELY SOLUTION

LEAVE BEHIND OLD SOLUTIONS

NOT IF YOU'RE ALONE

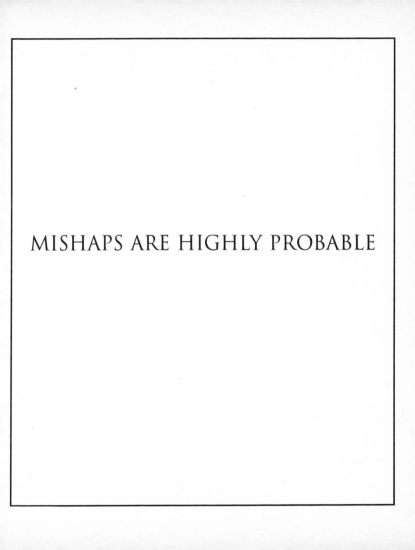

MISHAPS ARE HIGHLY PROBABLE

PRESS FOR CLOSURE

REALIZE THAT
TOO MANY CHOICES IS AS
DIFFICULT AS TOO FEW

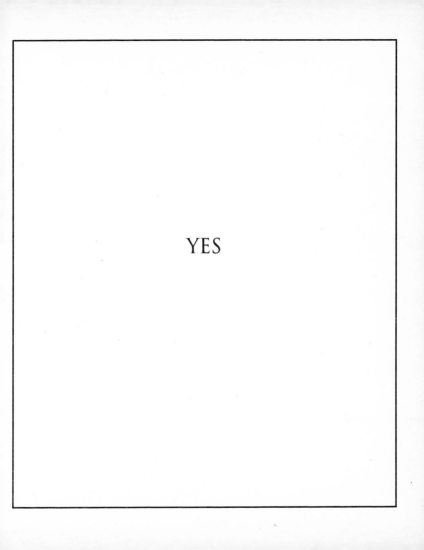

YES

LISTEN MORE CAREFULLY;
THEN YOU WILL KNOW

THE ANSWER
IS IN YOUR BACKYARD

LAUGH ABOUT IT

OTHERS WILL DEPEND
ON YOUR CHOICES

LET IT GO

THAT WOULD BE A WASTE
OF MONEY

GIVE IT ALL YOU'VE GOT

YOU DON'T REALLY CARE

YOU'LL NEED TO
CONSIDER OTHER WAYS

A YEAR FROM NOW
IT WON'T MATTER

DON'T WASTE YOUR TIME

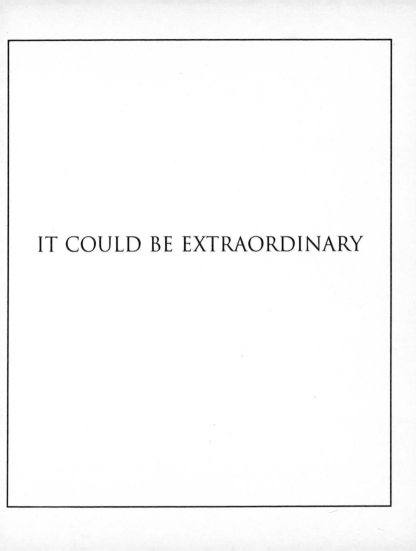

IT COULD BE EXTRAORDINARY

COUNT TO 10;
ASK AGAIN

ACT AS THOUGH
IT IS ALREADY REAL

SETTING PRIORITIES
WILL BE A NECESSARY PART
OF THE PROCESS

USE YOUR IMAGINATION

IT'S GOING TO BE GREAT

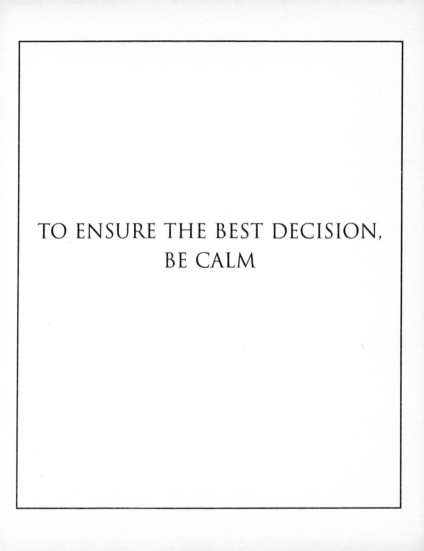

TO ENSURE THE BEST DECISION,
BE CALM

WAIT

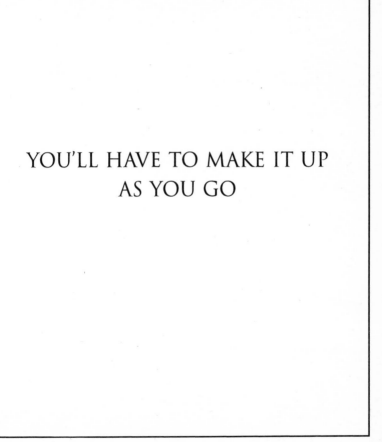

YOU'LL HAVE TO MAKE IT UP
AS YOU GO

YOU'LL REGRET IT

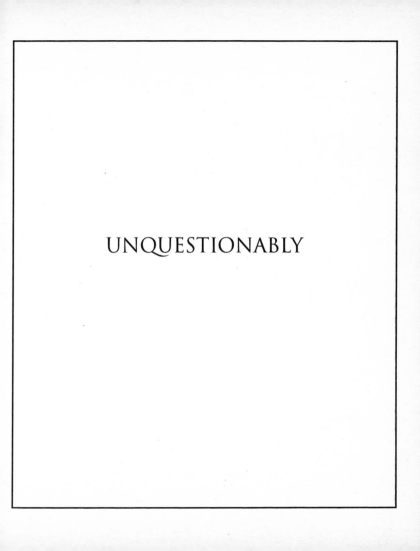

UNQUESTIONABLY

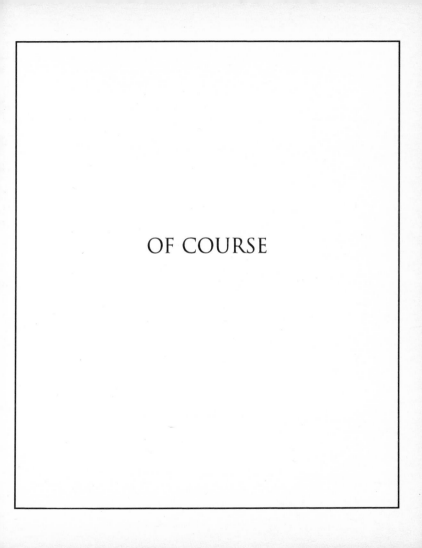

OF COURSE

YOU KNOW BETTER NOW
THAN EVER BEFORE

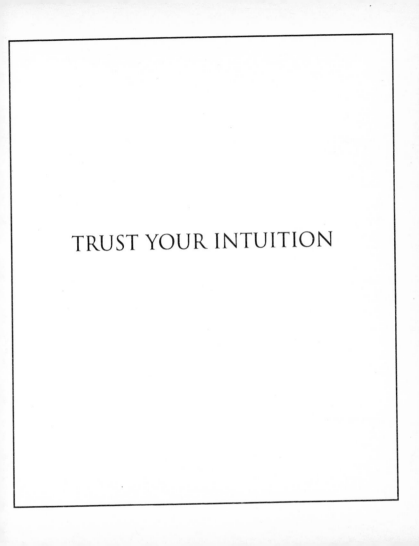

TRUST YOUR INTUITION

CONSIDER IT AN OPPORTUNITY

ASK YOUR FATHER

NEVER

ASK YOUR MOTHER

PERHAPS, WHEN YOU'RE OLDER

ONLY DO IT ONCE

MAYBE

NO

YES

YOUR ACTIONS WILL
IMPROVE THINGS

DON'T BE RIDICULOUS

DON'T BET ON IT

ADOPT
AN ADVENTUROUS ATTITUDE

FOLLOW THE ADVICE OF EXPERTS

YOU COULD FIND YOURSELF
UNABLE TO COMPROMISE

FOCUS ON YOUR HOME LIFE

INVESTIGATE
AND THEN ENJOY IT

DEFINITELY

IT WILL REMAIN UNPREDICTABLE

ABSOLUTELY NOT

EXPLORE IT
WITH PLAYFUL CURIOSITY

BE DELIGHTFULLY SURE OF IT

BETTER TO WAIT

IT SEEMS ASSURED

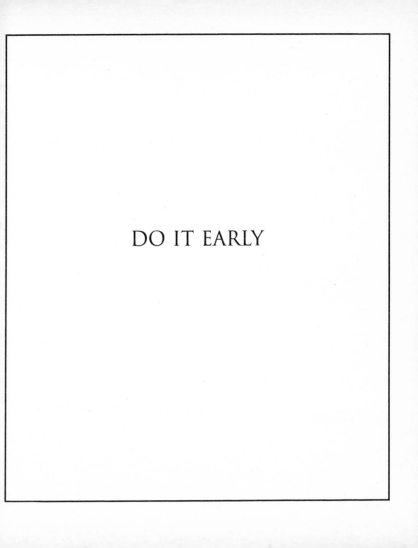

DO IT EARLY

KEEP IT TO YOURSELF

STARTLING EVENTS
MAY OCCUR AS A RESULT

THE ANSWER MAY COME TO YOU
IN ANOTHER LANGUAGE

YOU WILL NEED TO
ACCOMMODATE

DOUBT IT

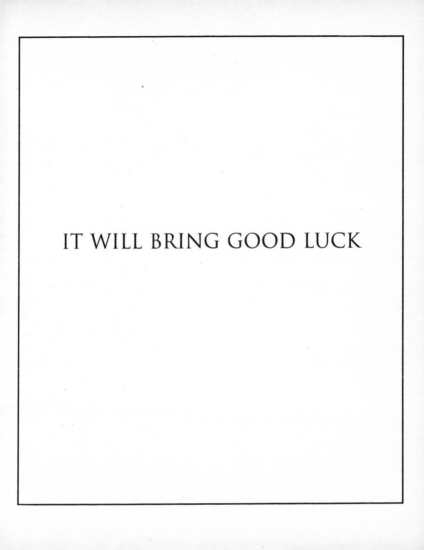

IT WILL BRING GOOD LUCK

BE PATIENT

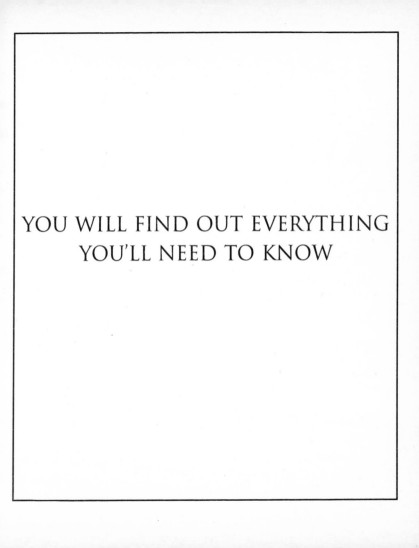

YOU WILL FIND OUT EVERYTHING
YOU'LL NEED TO KNOW

THERE IS A SUBSTANTIAL LINK
TO ANOTHER SITUATION

WATCH AND SEE WHAT HAPPENS

IT WILL AFFECT
HOW OTHERS SEE YOU

YOU'LL BE HAPPY YOU DID

GET IT IN WRITING

UNFAVOURABLE AT THIS TIME

UPGRADE ANY WAY YOU CAN

IF YOU DO AS YOU'RE TOLD

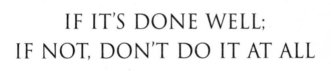

IF IT'S DONE WELL;
IF NOT, DON'T DO IT AT ALL

DON'T ASK FOR ANY MORE
AT THIS TIME

AVOID THE FIRST SOLUTION

YOU'LL GET THE FINAL WORD

PROCEED AT A MORE
RELAXED PACE

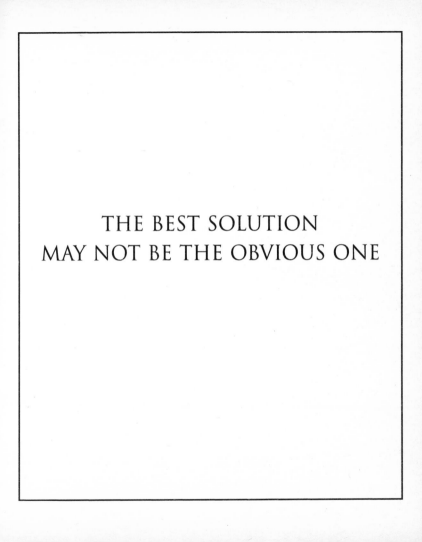

THE BEST SOLUTION
MAY NOT BE THE OBVIOUS ONE

REMAIN FLEXIBLE

THAT'S OUT OF YOUR CONTROL

PROVIDED YOU SAY
'THANK YOU'

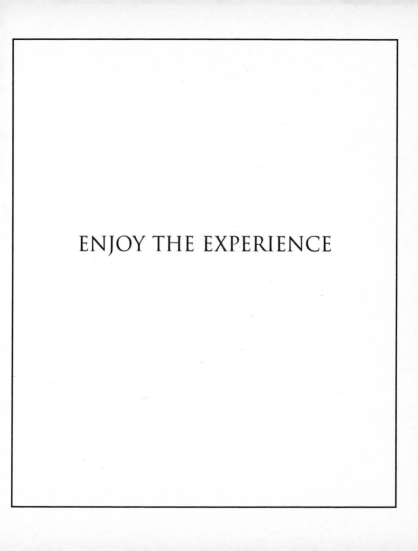

ENJOY THE EXPERIENCE

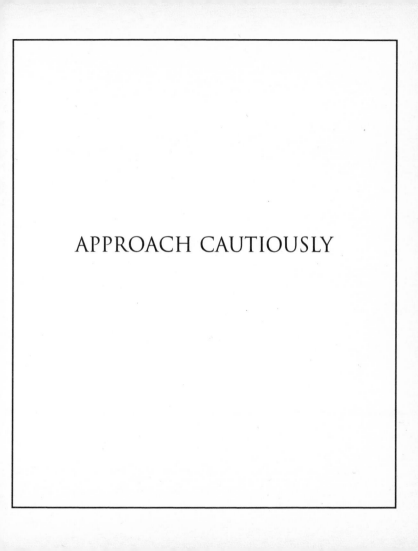

APPROACH CAUTIOUSLY

PAY ATTENTION TO THE DETAILS

WATCH YOUR STEP AS YOU GO

SPEAK UP ABOUT IT

DON'T HESITATE

THIS IS A GOOD TIME TO
MAKE A NEW PLAN

MOVE ON

THERE IS NO GUARANTEE

THE CIRCUMSTANCES
WILL CHANGE VERY QUICKLY

DON'T GET CAUGHT UP
IN YOUR EMOTIONS

SHIFT YOUR FOCUS

IT IS SIGNIFICANT

REPRIORITIZE WHAT
IS IMPORTANT

MAKE A LIST OF WHY NOT

DON'T WAIT

THERE IS GOOD REASON
TO BE OPTIMISTIC

IT IS SOMETHING
YOU WON'T FORGET

NO

SEEK OUT MORE OPTIONS

FOLLOW THROUGH
ON YOUR OBLIGATIONS

DEAL WITH IT LATER

FOLLOW SOMEONE ELSE'S LEAD

MAKE A LIST OF WHY

TAKE A CHANCE

ACCEPT A CHANGE
TO YOUR ROUTINE

YOU'LL NEED TO TAKE
THE INITIATIVE

YOU'LL HAVE TO COMPROMISE

YOU'LL NEED
MORE INFORMATION

TRUST YOUR
ORIGINAL THOUGHT

IT WILL CREATE A STIR

REMOVE YOUR OWN OBSTACLES

IT WOULD BE BETTER
TO FOCUS ON YOUR WORK

IT WILL BE A PLEASURE

BE MORE GENEROUS

BET ON IT

MISHAPS ARE HIGHLY PROBABLE

PRESS FOR CLOSURE

REALIZE THAT
TOO MANY CHOICES IS AS
DIFFICULT AS TOO FEW

YOU MUST

LISTEN MORE CAREFULLY;
THEN YOU WILL KNOW

THE ANSWER
IS IN YOUR BACKYARD

LAUGH ABOUT IT

OTHERS WILL DEPEND
ON YOUR CHOICES

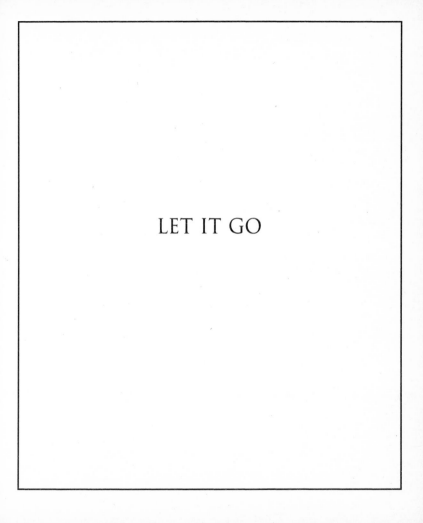

LET IT GO

THAT WOULD BE A WASTE
OF MONEY

IT'S TIME FOR YOU TO GO

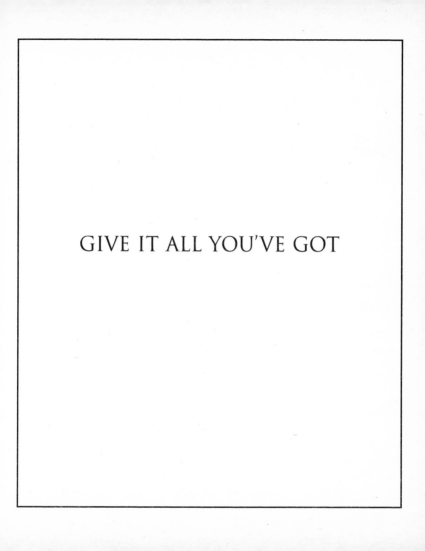

GIVE IT ALL YOU'VE GOT

YOU DON'T REALLY CARE

YOU'LL NEED TO
CONSIDER OTHER WAYS

A YEAR FROM NOW
IT WON'T MATTER

DON'T WASTE YOUR TIME

IT COULD BE EXTRAORDINARY

COUNT TO 10;
ASK AGAIN

ACT AS THOUGH
IT IS ALREADY REAL

SETTING PRIORITIES
WILL BE A NECESSARY PART
OF THE PROCESS

USE YOUR IMAGINATION

IT'S GOING TO BE GREAT

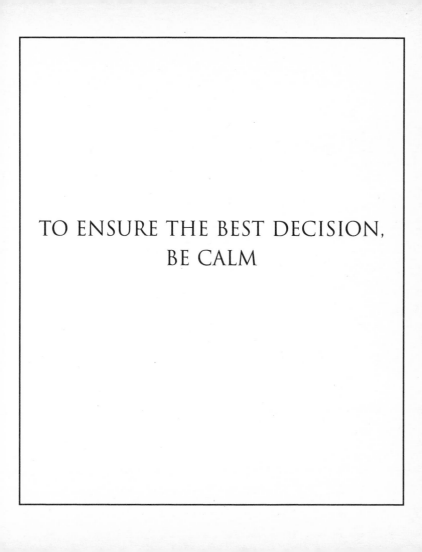

TO ENSURE THE BEST DECISION,
BE CALM

WAIT

YOU'LL HAVE TO MAKE IT UP
AS YOU GO

YOU'LL REGRET IT

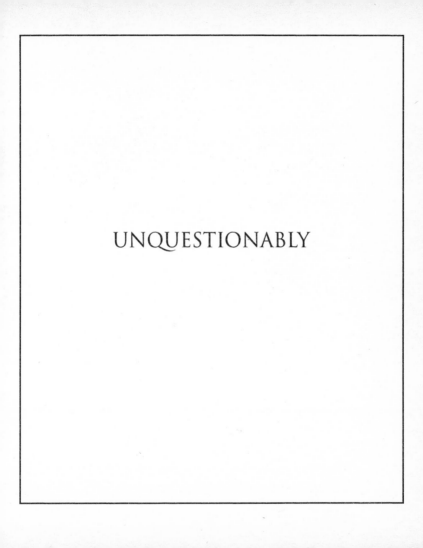

UNQUESTIONABLY

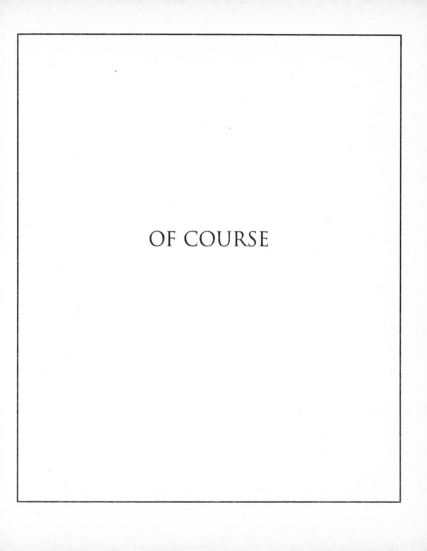

OF COURSE

YOU KNOW BETTER NOW
THAN EVER BEFORE

TRUST YOUR INTUITION

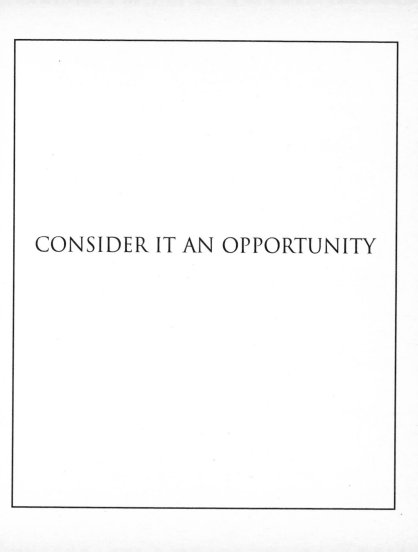

CONSIDER IT AN OPPORTUNITY

ASK YOUR FATHER

NEVER

ASK YOUR MOTHER

PERHAPS, WHEN YOU'RE OLDER

ONLY DO IT ONCE

MAYBE

NO

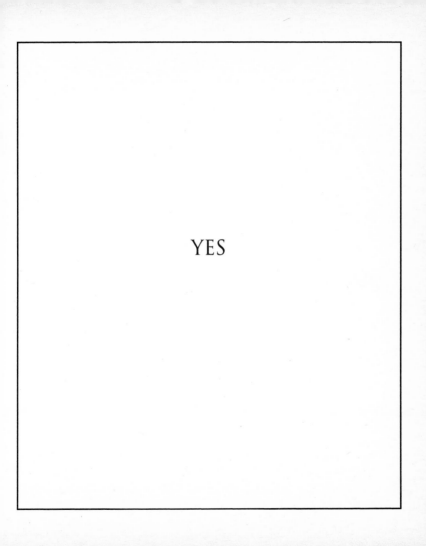

YES

FINISH SOMETHING ELSE FIRST

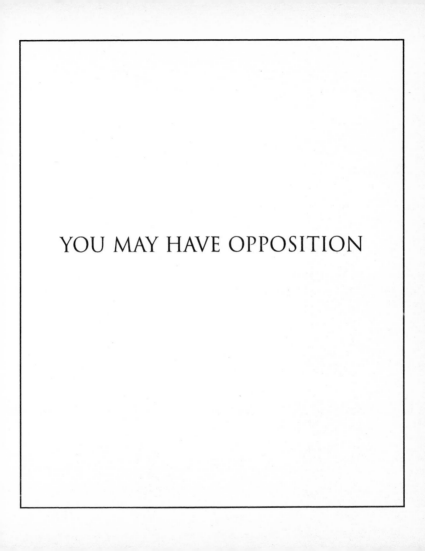

YOU MAY HAVE OPPOSITION

YOU ARE TOO CLOSE TO SEE

THE SITUATION IS UNCLEAR

A SUBSTANTIAL EFFORT
WILL BE REQUIRED

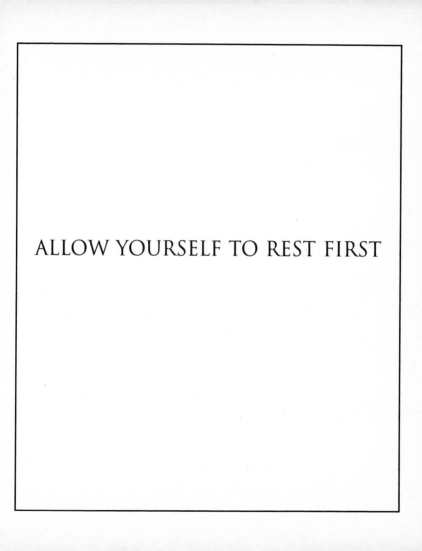

ALLOW YOURSELF TO REST FIRST

THE CHANCE WILL NOT
COME AGAIN SOON

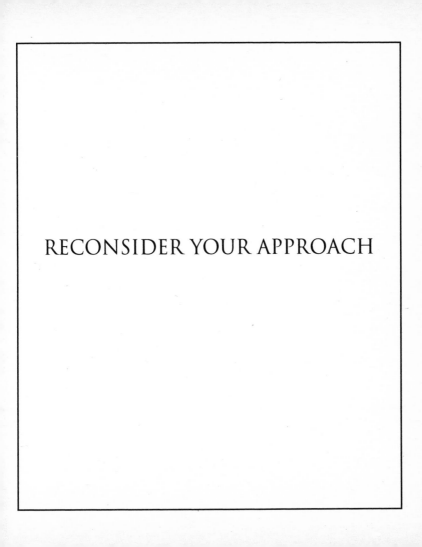

RECONSIDER YOUR APPROACH

IT WOULD BE INADVISABLE

WAIT FOR A BETTER OFFER

SETTLE IT SOON

YES,
BUT DON'T FORCE IT

GET A CLEARER VIEW

TAKE A CHANCE

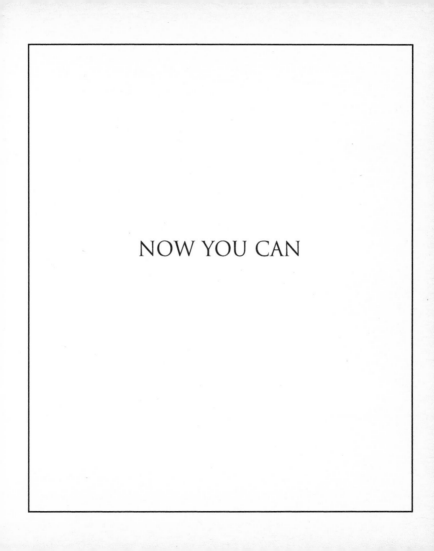

NOW YOU CAN

DON'T OVERDO IT

IT WILL SUSTAIN YOU

IT'LL COST YOU

IT IS SURE TO MAKE THINGS
INTERESTING

BE PRACTICAL

SAVE YOUR ENERGY

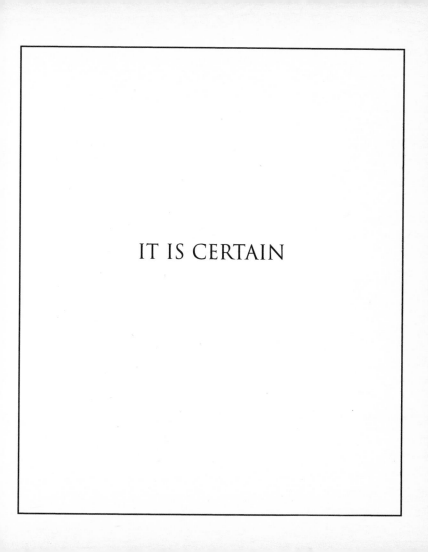

IT IS CERTAIN

IT IS UNCERTAIN

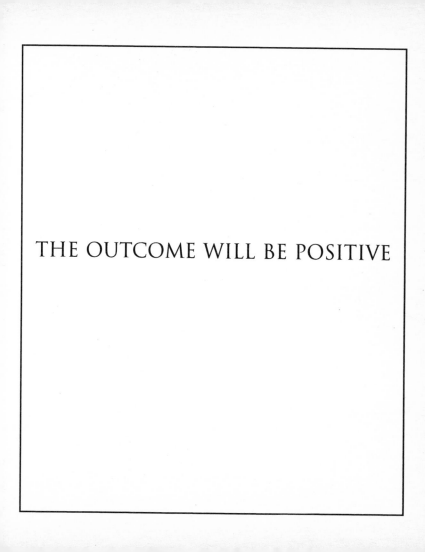

THE OUTCOME WILL BE POSITIVE

NO MATTER WHAT

YOU MAY HAVE TO DROP
OTHER THINGS

DON'T BE CONCERNED

PREPARE FOR THE UNEXPECTED

IT IS NOT SIGNIFICANT

TELL SOMEONE
WHAT IT MEANS TO YOU

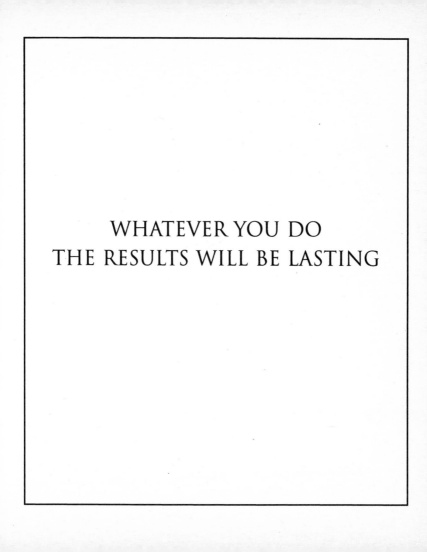

WHATEVER YOU DO
THE RESULTS WILL BE LASTING

KEEP AN OPEN MIND

IT'S A GOOD TIME
TO MAKE PLANS

IT MAY BE DIFFICULT
BUT YOU WILL FIND VALUE IN IT

IT IS WORTH THE TROUBLE

THERE WILL BE OBSTACLES
TO OVERCOME

RELATED ISSUES MAY SURFACE

YOU ARE SURE TO HAVE SUPPORT

ASSISTANCE WOULD MAKE
YOUR PROGRESS
A SUCCESS

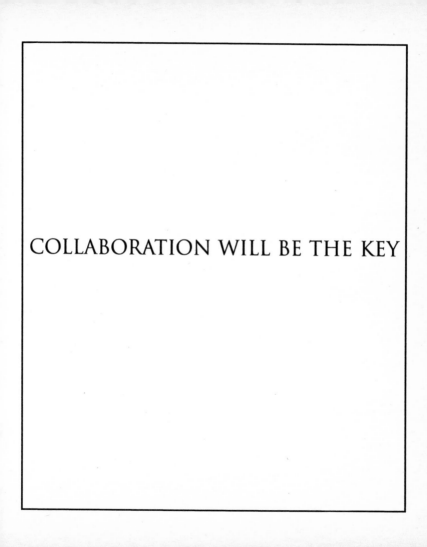

COLLABORATION WILL BE THE KEY

SEEK OUT MORE OPTIONS

TAKE CHARGE

IT CANNOT FAIL

YOU MUST ACT NOW

RESPECT THE RULES

GENTLE PERSISTENCE
WILL PAY OFF

YOU WILL BE DISAPPOINTED

IT MAY ALREADY BE
A DONE DEAL

FOLLOW THROUGH
WITH YOUR GOOD INTENTIONS

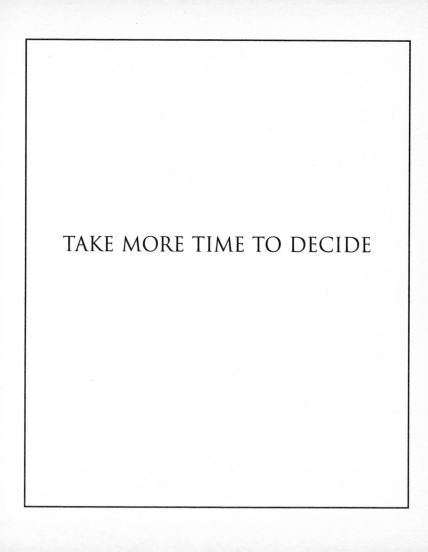

TAKE MORE TIME TO DECIDE

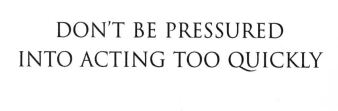

DON'T BE PRESSURED
INTO ACTING TOO QUICKLY

DON'T IGNORE THE OBVIOUS

IF YOU DON'T RESIST

IT'S NOT WORTH A STRUGGLE

DON'T FORGET TO HAVE FUN

DON'T DOUBT IT

A STRONG COMMITMENT
WILL ACHIEVE GOOD RESULTS

TRY A MORE UNLIKELY SOLUTION

LEAVE BEHIND OLD SOLUTIONS

NOT IF YOU'RE ALONE

ACKNOWLEDGEMENTS

From the start, the support for *The Book of Answers* has been overwhelming; and so the list of people who I thank for their support is much longer than I can fit on this page. However, there are a handful who are truly special to me and to this book's evolution:

My mother and father, Doris and Bob, who have always provided me with the right answers . . . thank you.

My confidant and after-hours editor, Kris.

My friend, Sandra, for her input and ongoing support.

My island parents, Reg and Larry, who are as generous with support as they are with sincerely good times.

My literary agent, Victoria Sanders, who has the enthusiasm, leadership, and good sense of several . . . thank you for believing and following through.

My editor, Jennifer Lang, for managing all the niggly details and still finding a fresh enthusiasm.

And to my Seattle support, the list is as long as it is deep: a double tall latte of thank yous! With special gratefuls and foam to Jaq, Tim, Martha, Michael, Joshua, Barbara, Maureen, Renee, and all the staff at Boat St. Cafe.